RESTAURANT
REVIEW JOURNAL

This Belongs To:

Restaurant Name:

Location/Address:

Contact Details/Social Media:

Cuisine/Type Of Food:

Dined With:

Signature Dishes:

Ambience Notes

Rating: ☆☆☆☆☆

Drinks/Cocktails Notes

Rating: ☆☆☆☆☆

Appetizer Notes

....

....

....

....

....

Rating: ☆☆☆☆☆

Main Course Notes

....

....

....

....

....

Rating: ☆☆☆☆☆

Desserts Note

....

....

....

....

....

Rating: ☆☆☆☆☆

Restaurant Name:

....

Location/Address:

....

Contact Details/Social Media:

....

Cuisine/Type Of Food:

....

Dined With:

....

Signature Dishes:

....

Ambience Notes

....

....

....

....

....

Rating: ☆☆☆☆☆

Drinks/Cocktails Notes

....

....

....

....

....

Rating: ☆☆☆☆☆

Appetizer Notes

....

....

....

....

....

Rating: ☆☆☆☆☆

Main Course Notes

....

....

....

....

....

Rating: ☆☆☆☆☆

Desserts Note

....

....

....

....

....

Rating: ☆☆☆☆☆

Restaurant Name:

Location/Address:

Contact Details/Social Media:

Cuisine/Type Of Food:

Dined With:

Signature Dishes:

Ambience Notes

Rating: ☆☆☆☆☆

Drinks/Cocktails Notes

Rating: ☆☆☆☆☆

Appetizer Notes

....

....

....

....

Rating: ☆☆☆☆☆

Main Course Notes

....

....

....

....

Rating: ☆☆☆☆☆

Desserts Note

....

....

....

....

....

Rating: ☆☆☆☆☆

Restaurant Name:

Location/Address:

Contact Details/Social Media:

Cuisine/Type Of Food:

Dined With:

Signature Dishes:

Ambience Notes

Rating: ☆☆☆☆☆

Drinks/Cocktails Notes

Rating: ☆☆☆☆☆

Appetizer Notes

....

....

....

....

....

Rating: ☆☆☆☆☆

Main Course Notes

....

....

....

....

....

Rating: ☆☆☆☆☆

Desserts Note

....

....

....

....

....

Rating: ☆☆☆☆☆

Restaurant Name:

Location/Address:

Contact Details/Social Media:

Cuisine/Type Of Food:

Dined With:

Signature Dishes:

Ambience Notes

Rating: ☆☆☆☆☆

Drinks/Cocktails Notes

Rating: ☆☆☆☆☆

Appetizer Notes

....

....

....

....

....

Rating: ☆☆☆☆☆

Main Course Notes

....

....

....

....

....

Rating: ☆☆☆☆☆

Desserts Note

....

....

....

....

....

Rating: ☆☆☆☆☆

Restaurant Name:

Location/Address:

Contact Details/Social Media:

Cuisine/Type Of Food:

Dined With:

Signature Dishes:

Ambience Notes

Rating: ☆☆☆☆☆

Drinks/Cocktails Notes

Rating: ☆☆☆☆☆

Appetizer Notes

....

....

....

....

....

Rating: ☆☆☆☆☆

Main Course Notes

....

....

....

....

....

Rating: ☆☆☆☆☆

Desserts Note

....

....

....

....

....

Rating: ☆☆☆☆☆

Restaurant Name:

Location/Address:

Contact Details/Social Media:

Cuisine/Type Of Food:

Dined With:

Signature Dishes:

Ambience Notes

Rating: ☆☆☆☆☆

Drinks/Cocktails Notes

Rating: ☆☆☆☆☆

Appetizer Notes

....

....

....

....

Rating: ☆☆☆☆☆

Main Course Notes

....

....

....

....

Rating: ☆☆☆☆☆

Desserts Note

....

....

....

....

Rating: ☆☆☆☆☆

Restaurant Name:

Location/Address:

Contact Details/Social Media:

Cuisine/Type Of Food:

Dined With:

Signature Dishes:

Ambience Notes

Rating: ☆☆☆☆☆

Drinks/Cocktails Notes

Rating: ☆☆☆☆☆

Appetizer Notes

....

....

....

....

....

Rating: ☆☆☆☆☆

Main Course Notes

....

....

....

....

....

Rating: ☆☆☆☆☆

Desserts Note

....

....

....

....

....

Rating: ☆☆☆☆☆

Restaurant Name:

Location/Address:

Contact Details/Social Media:

Cuisine/Type Of Food:

Dined With:

Signature Dishes:

Ambience Notes

Rating: ☆☆☆☆☆

Drinks/Cocktails Notes

Rating: ☆☆☆☆☆

Appetizer Notes

....

....

....

....

....

Rating: ☆☆☆☆☆

Main Course Notes

....

....

....

....

....

Rating: ☆☆☆☆☆

Desserts Note

....

....

....

....

....

Rating: ☆☆☆☆☆

Restaurant Name:

Location/Address:

Contact Details/Social Media:

Cuisine/Type Of Food:

Dined With:

Signature Dishes:

Ambience Notes

Rating: ☆☆☆☆☆

Drinks/Cocktails Notes

Rating: ☆☆☆☆☆

Appetizer Notes

....

....

....

....

....

Rating: ☆☆☆☆☆

Main Course Notes

....

....

....

....

....

Rating: ☆☆☆☆☆

Desserts Note

....

....

....

....

....

Rating: ☆☆☆☆☆

Restaurant Name:

Location/Address:

Contact Details/Social Media:

Cuisine/Type Of Food:

Dined With:

Signature Dishes:

Ambience Notes

Rating: ☆☆☆☆☆

Drinks/Cocktails Notes

Rating: ☆☆☆☆☆

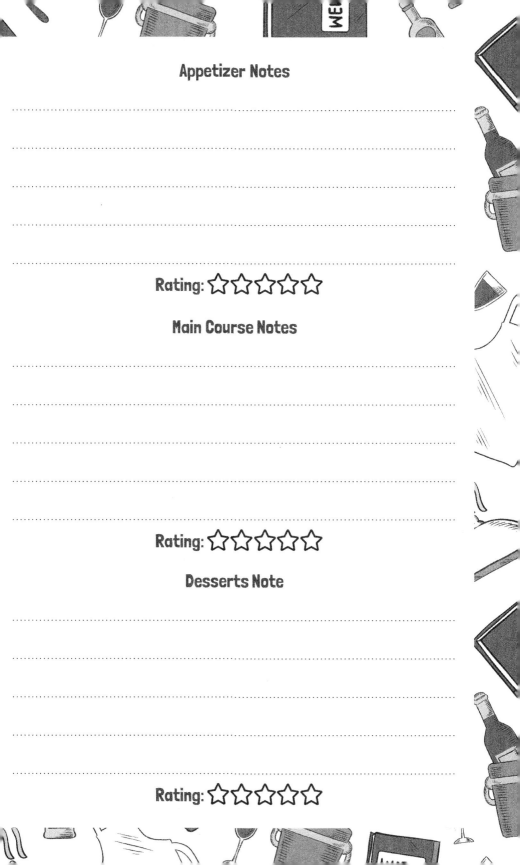

Appetizer Notes

....

....

....

....

....

Rating: ☆☆☆☆☆

Main Course Notes

....

....

....

....

....

Rating: ☆☆☆☆☆

Desserts Note

....

....

....

....

....

Rating: ☆☆☆☆☆

Restaurant Name:

Location/Address:

Contact Details/Social Media:

Cuisine/Type Of Food:

Dined With:

Signature Dishes:

Ambience Notes

Rating: ☆☆☆☆☆

Drinks/Cocktails Notes

Rating: ☆☆☆☆☆

Appetizer Notes

....

....

....

....

....

Rating: ☆☆☆☆☆

Main Course Notes

....

....

....

....

....

Rating: ☆☆☆☆☆

Desserts Note

....

....

....

....

....

Rating: ☆☆☆☆☆

Restaurant Name:

Location/Address:

Contact Details/Social Media:

Cuisine/Type Of Food:

Dined With:

Signature Dishes:

Ambience Notes

Rating: ☆☆☆☆☆

Drinks/Cocktails Notes

Rating: ☆☆☆☆☆

Appetizer Notes

....

....

....

....

....

Rating: ☆☆☆☆☆

Main Course Notes

....

....

....

....

....

Rating: ☆☆☆☆☆

Desserts Note

....

....

....

....

....

Rating: ☆☆☆☆☆

Restaurant Name:

Location/Address:

Contact Details/Social Media:

Cuisine/Type Of Food:

Dined With:

Signature Dishes:

Ambience Notes

Rating: ☆☆☆☆☆

Drinks/Cocktails Notes

Rating: ☆☆☆☆☆

Appetizer Notes

....

....

....

....

....

Rating: ☆☆☆☆☆

Main Course Notes

....

....

....

....

....

Rating: ☆☆☆☆☆

Desserts Note

....

....

....

....

....

Rating: ☆☆☆☆☆

Restaurant Name:

Location/Address:

Contact Details/Social Media:

Cuisine/Type Of Food:

Dined With:

Signature Dishes:

Ambience Notes

Rating: ☆☆☆☆☆

Drinks/Cocktails Notes

Rating: ☆☆☆☆☆

Appetizer Notes

....

....

....

....

Rating: ☆☆☆☆☆

Main Course Notes

....

....

....

....

Rating: ☆☆☆☆☆

Desserts Note

....

....

....

....

....

Rating: ☆☆☆☆☆

Restaurant Name:

Location/Address:

Contact Details/Social Media:

Cuisine/Type Of Food:

Dined With:

Signature Dishes:

Ambience Notes

Rating: ☆☆☆☆☆

Drinks/Cocktails Notes

Rating: ☆☆☆☆☆

Appetizer Notes

....

....

....

....

....

Rating: ☆☆☆☆☆

Main Course Notes

....

....

....

....

....

Rating: ☆☆☆☆☆

Desserts Note

....

....

....

....

....

Rating: ☆☆☆☆☆

Restaurant Name:

Location/Address:

Contact Details/Social Media:

Cuisine/Type Of Food:

Dined With:

Signature Dishes:

Ambience Notes

Rating: ☆☆☆☆☆

Drinks/Cocktails Notes

Rating: ☆☆☆☆☆

Appetizer Notes

....

....

....

....

....

Rating: ☆☆☆☆☆

Main Course Notes

....

....

....

....

....

Rating: ☆☆☆☆☆

Desserts Note

....

....

....

....

....

Rating: ☆☆☆☆☆

Restaurant Name:

Location/Address:

Contact Details/Social Media:

Cuisine/Type Of Food:

Dined With:

Signature Dishes:

Ambience Notes

Rating: ☆☆☆☆☆

Drinks/Cocktails Notes

Rating: ☆☆☆☆☆

Appetizer Notes

....

....

....

....

....

Rating: ☆☆☆☆☆

Main Course Notes

....

....

....

....

....

Rating: ☆☆☆☆☆

Desserts Note

....

....

....

....

....

Rating: ☆☆☆☆☆

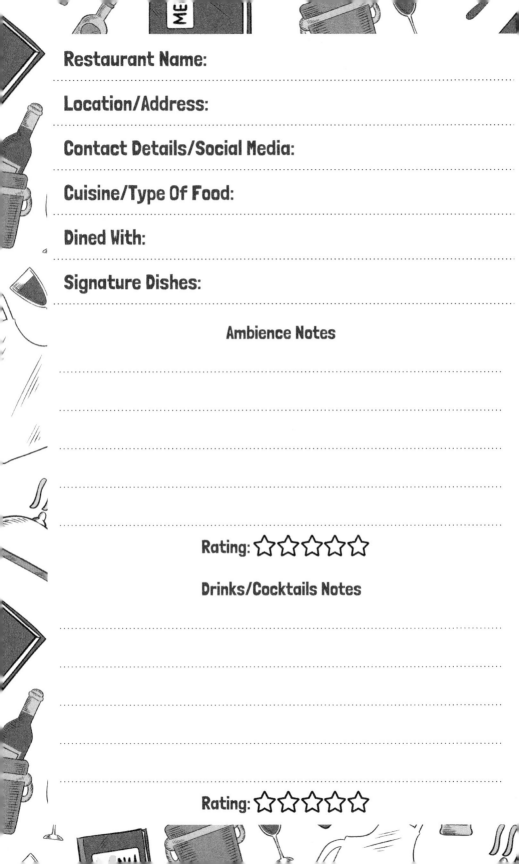

Restaurant Name:

Location/Address:

Contact Details/Social Media:

Cuisine/Type Of Food:

Dined With:

Signature Dishes:

Ambience Notes

Rating: ☆☆☆☆☆

Drinks/Cocktails Notes

Rating: ☆☆☆☆☆

Appetizer Notes

....

....

....

....

....

Rating: ☆☆☆☆☆

Main Course Notes

....

....

....

....

....

Rating: ☆☆☆☆☆

Desserts Note

....

....

....

....

....

Rating: ☆☆☆☆☆

Restaurant Name:

....

Location/Address:

....

Contact Details/Social Media:

....

Cuisine/Type Of Food:

....

Dined With:

....

Signature Dishes:

....

Ambience Notes

....

....

....

....

Rating: ☆☆☆☆☆

Drinks/Cocktails Notes

....

....

....

....

....

Rating: ☆☆☆☆☆

Appetizer Notes

....

....

....

....

....

Rating: ☆☆☆☆☆

Main Course Notes

....

....

....

....

....

Rating: ☆☆☆☆☆

Desserts Note

....

....

....

....

....

Rating: ☆☆☆☆☆

Restaurant Name:

Location/Address:

Contact Details/Social Media:

Cuisine/Type Of Food:

Dined With:

Signature Dishes:

Ambience Notes

Rating: ☆☆☆☆☆

Drinks/Cocktails Notes

Rating: ☆☆☆☆☆

Appetizer Notes

....

....

....

....

....

Rating: ☆☆☆☆☆

Main Course Notes

....

....

....

....

....

Rating: ☆☆☆☆☆

Desserts Note

....

....

....

....

....

Rating: ☆☆☆☆☆

Restaurant Name:

Location/Address:

Contact Details/Social Media:

Cuisine/Type Of Food:

Dined With:

Signature Dishes:

Ambience Notes

Rating: ☆☆☆☆☆

Drinks/Cocktails Notes

Rating: ☆☆☆☆☆

Appetizer Notes

....

....

....

....

....

Rating: ☆☆☆☆☆

Main Course Notes

....

....

....

....

....

Rating: ☆☆☆☆☆

Desserts Note

....

....

....

....

....

Rating: ☆☆☆☆☆

Restaurant Name:

Location/Address:

Contact Details/Social Media:

Cuisine/Type Of Food:

Dined With:

Signature Dishes:

Ambience Notes

Rating: ☆☆☆☆☆

Drinks/Cocktails Notes

Rating: ☆☆☆☆☆

Appetizer Notes

....

....

....

....

Rating: ☆☆☆☆☆

Main Course Notes

....

....

....

....

Rating: ☆☆☆☆☆

Desserts Note

....

....

....

....

....

Rating: ☆☆☆☆☆

Restaurant Name:

Location/Address:

Contact Details/Social Media:

Cuisine/Type Of Food:

Dined With:

Signature Dishes:

Ambience Notes

Rating: ☆☆☆☆☆

Drinks/Cocktails Notes

Rating: ☆☆☆☆☆

Appetizer Notes

....

....

....

....

....

Rating: ☆☆☆☆☆

Main Course Notes

....

....

....

....

....

Rating: ☆☆☆☆☆

Desserts Note

....

....

....

....

....

Rating: ☆☆☆☆☆

Restaurant Name:

....

Location/Address:

....

Contact Details/Social Media:

....

Cuisine/Type Of Food:

....

Dined With:

....

Signature Dishes:

....

Ambience Notes

....

....

....

....

....

Rating: ☆☆☆☆☆

Drinks/Cocktails Notes

....

....

....

....

....

Rating: ☆☆☆☆☆

Appetizer Notes

....

....

....

....

....

Rating: ☆☆☆☆☆

Main Course Notes

....

....

....

....

....

Rating: ☆☆☆☆☆

Desserts Note

....

....

....

....

....

Rating: ☆☆☆☆☆

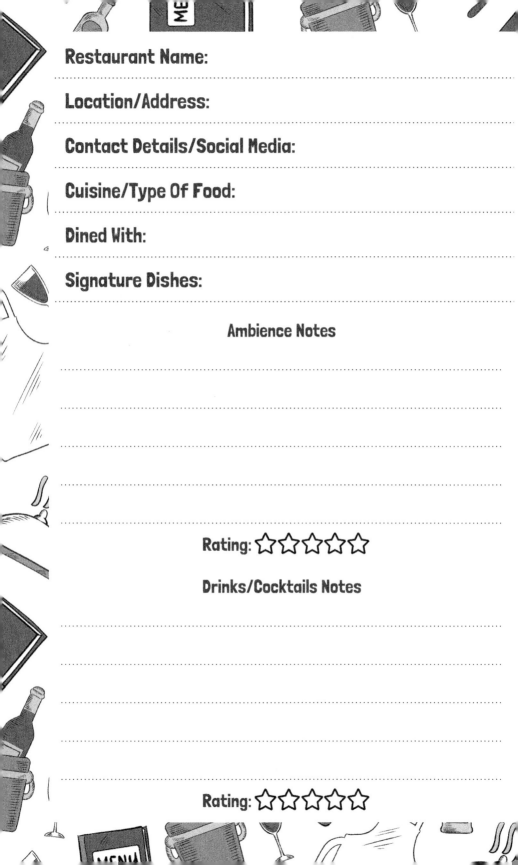

Restaurant Name:

Location/Address:

Contact Details/Social Media:

Cuisine/Type Of Food:

Dined With:

Signature Dishes:

Ambience Notes

Rating: ☆☆☆☆☆

Drinks/Cocktails Notes

Rating: ☆☆☆☆☆

Appetizer Notes

....

....

....

....

....

Rating: ☆☆☆☆☆

Main Course Notes

....

....

....

....

....

Rating: ☆☆☆☆☆

Desserts Note

....

....

....

....

....

Rating: ☆☆☆☆☆

Restaurant Name:

Location/Address:

Contact Details/Social Media:

Cuisine/Type Of Food:

Dined With:

Signature Dishes:

Ambience Notes

Rating: ☆☆☆☆☆

Drinks/Cocktails Notes

Rating: ☆☆☆☆☆

Appetizer Notes

....

....

....

....

....

Rating: ☆☆☆☆☆

Main Course Notes

....

....

....

....

....

Rating: ☆☆☆☆☆

Desserts Note

....

....

....

....

....

Rating: ☆☆☆☆☆

Restaurant Name:

Location/Address:

Contact Details/Social Media:

Cuisine/Type Of Food:

Dined With:

Signature Dishes:

Ambience Notes

Rating: ☆☆☆☆☆

Drinks/Cocktails Notes

Rating: ☆☆☆☆☆

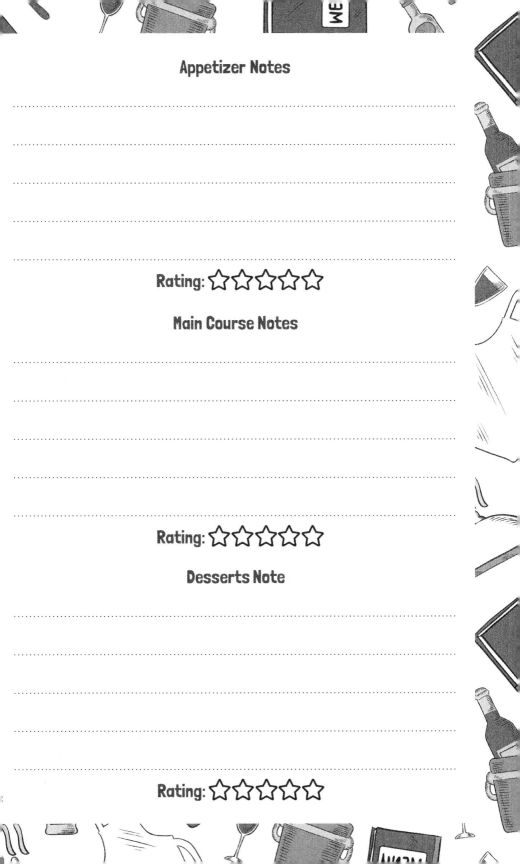

Appetizer Notes

....

....

....

....

....

Rating: ☆☆☆☆☆

Main Course Notes

....

....

....

....

....

Rating: ☆☆☆☆☆

Desserts Note

....

....

....

....

....

Rating: ☆☆☆☆☆

Restaurant Name:

....

Location/Address:

....

Contact Details/Social Media:

....

Cuisine/Type Of Food:

....

Dined With:

....

Signature Dishes:

....

Ambience Notes

....

....

....

....

....

Rating: ☆☆☆☆☆

Drinks/Cocktails Notes

....

....

....

....

....

Rating: ☆☆☆☆☆

Appetizer Notes

....

....

....

....

Rating: ☆☆☆☆☆

Main Course Notes

....

....

....

....

Rating: ☆☆☆☆☆

Desserts Note

....

....

....

....

....

Rating: ☆☆☆☆☆

Restaurant Name:

Location/Address:

Contact Details/Social Media:

Cuisine/Type Of Food:

Dined With:

Signature Dishes:

Ambience Notes

Rating: ☆☆☆☆☆

Drinks/Cocktails Notes

Rating: ☆☆☆☆☆

Appetizer Notes

....

....

....

....

....

Rating: ☆☆☆☆☆

Main Course Notes

....

....

....

....

....

Rating: ☆☆☆☆☆

Desserts Note

....

....

....

....

....

Rating: ☆☆☆☆☆

Restaurant Name:

Location/Address:

Contact Details/Social Media:

Cuisine/Type Of Food:

Dined With:

Signature Dishes:

Ambience Notes

Rating: ☆☆☆☆☆

Drinks/Cocktails Notes

Rating: ☆☆☆☆☆

Appetizer Notes

....

....

....

....

....

Rating: ☆☆☆☆☆

Main Course Notes

....

....

....

....

....

Rating: ☆☆☆☆☆

Desserts Note

....

....

....

....

....

Rating: ☆☆☆☆☆

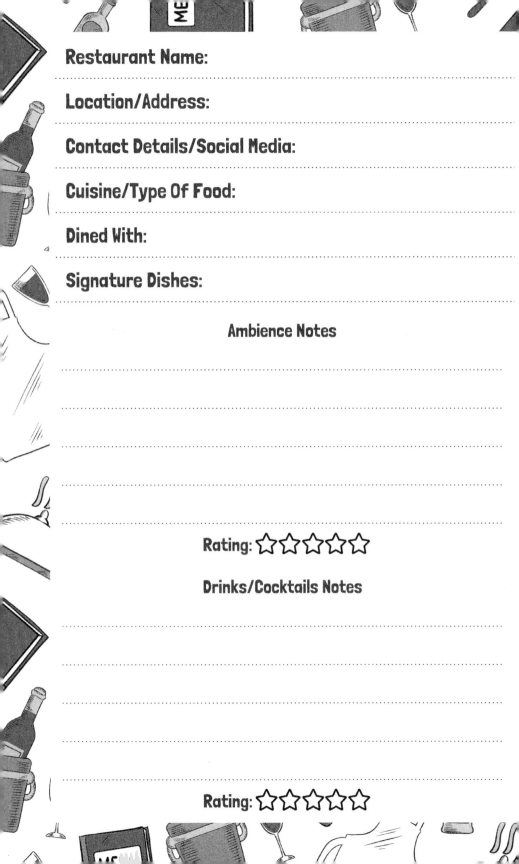

Restaurant Name:

Location/Address:

Contact Details/Social Media:

Cuisine/Type Of Food:

Dined With:

Signature Dishes:

Ambience Notes

Rating: ☆☆☆☆☆

Drinks/Cocktails Notes

Rating: ☆☆☆☆☆

Appetizer Notes

....

....

....

....

....

Rating: ☆☆☆☆☆

Main Course Notes

....

....

....

....

....

Rating: ☆☆☆☆☆

Desserts Note

....

....

....

....

....

Rating: ☆☆☆☆☆

Restaurant Name:

Location/Address:

Contact Details/Social Media:

Cuisine/Type Of Food:

Dined With:

Signature Dishes:

Ambience Notes

Rating: ☆☆☆☆☆

Drinks/Cocktails Notes

Rating: ☆☆☆☆☆

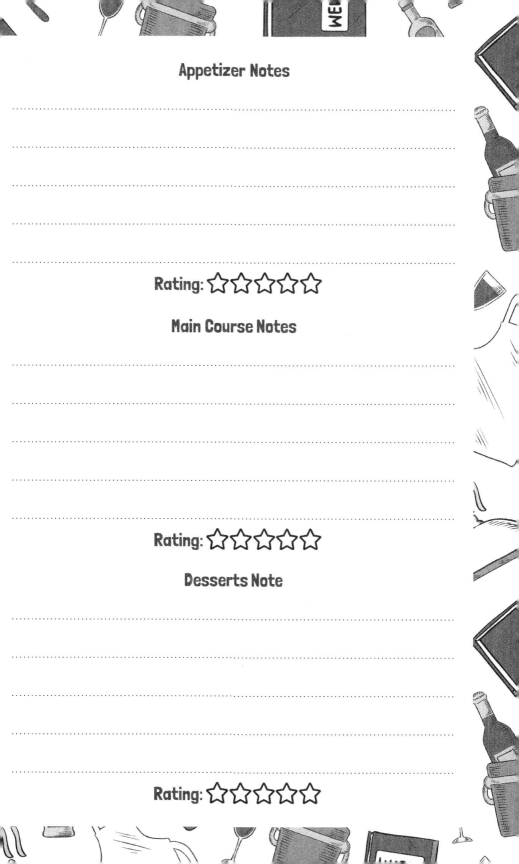

Appetizer Notes

....

....

....

....

....

Rating: ☆☆☆☆☆

Main Course Notes

....

....

....

....

....

Rating: ☆☆☆☆☆

Desserts Note

....

....

....

....

....

Rating: ☆☆☆☆☆

Restaurant Name:

Location/Address:

Contact Details/Social Media:

Cuisine/Type Of Food:

Dined With:

Signature Dishes:

Ambience Notes

Rating: ☆☆☆☆☆

Drinks/Cocktails Notes

Rating: ☆☆☆☆☆

Appetizer Notes

....

....

....

....

....

Rating: ☆☆☆☆☆

Main Course Notes

....

....

....

....

....

Rating: ☆☆☆☆☆

Desserts Note

....

....

....

....

....

Rating: ☆☆☆☆☆

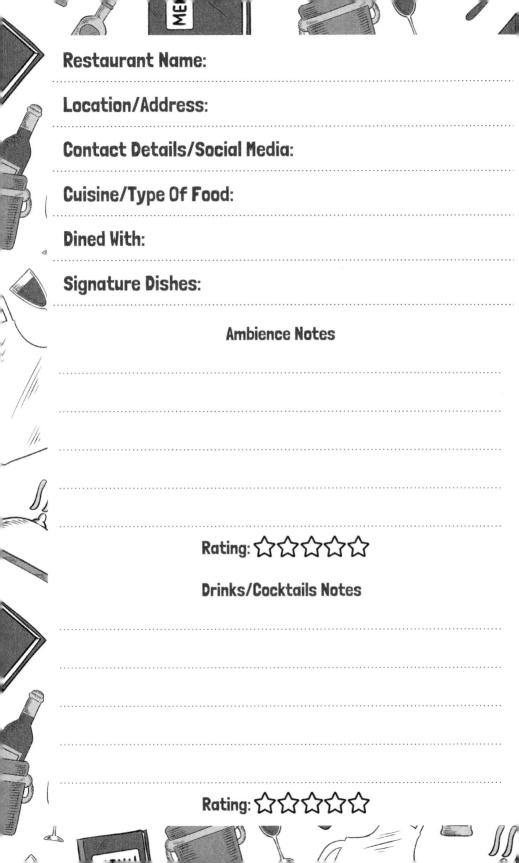

Restaurant Name:

Location/Address:

Contact Details/Social Media:

Cuisine/Type Of Food:

Dined With:

Signature Dishes:

Ambience Notes

Rating: ☆☆☆☆☆

Drinks/Cocktails Notes

Rating: ☆☆☆☆☆

Appetizer Notes

....

....

....

....

....

Rating: ☆☆☆☆☆

Main Course Notes

....

....

....

....

....

Rating: ☆☆☆☆☆

Desserts Note

....

....

....

....

....

Rating: ☆☆☆☆☆

Restaurant Name:

Location/Address:

Contact Details/Social Media:

Cuisine/Type Of Food:

Dined With:

Signature Dishes:

Ambience Notes

Rating: ☆☆☆☆☆

Drinks/Cocktails Notes

Rating: ☆☆☆☆☆

Appetizer Notes

....

....

....

....

....

Rating: ☆☆☆☆☆

Main Course Notes

....

....

....

....

....

Rating: ☆☆☆☆☆

Desserts Note

....

....

....

....

....

Rating: ☆☆☆☆☆

Restaurant Name:

Location/Address:

Contact Details/Social Media:

Cuisine/Type Of Food:

Dined With:

Signature Dishes:

Ambience Notes

Rating: ☆☆☆☆☆

Drinks/Cocktails Notes

Rating: ☆☆☆☆☆

Appetizer Notes

....
....
....
....
....

Rating: ☆☆☆☆☆

Main Course Notes

....
....
....
....

Rating: ☆☆☆☆☆

Desserts Note

....
....
....
....
....

Rating: ☆☆☆☆☆

Restaurant Name:

Location/Address:

Contact Details/Social Media:

Cuisine/Type Of Food:

Dined With:

Signature Dishes:

Ambience Notes

Rating: ☆☆☆☆☆

Drinks/Cocktails Notes

Rating: ☆☆☆☆☆

Appetizer Notes

....

....

....

....

....

Rating: ☆☆☆☆☆

Main Course Notes

....

....

....

....

....

Rating: ☆☆☆☆☆

Desserts Note

....

....

....

....

....

Rating: ☆☆☆☆☆

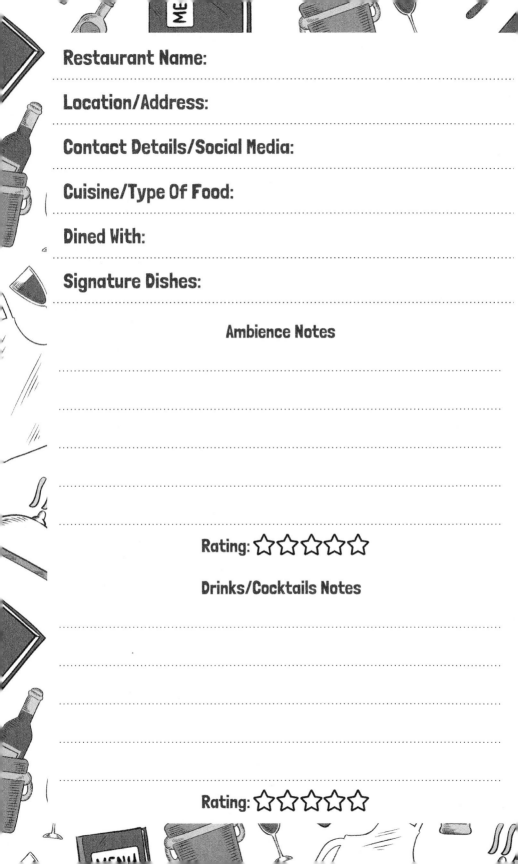

Restaurant Name:

Location/Address:

Contact Details/Social Media:

Cuisine/Type Of Food:

Dined With:

Signature Dishes:

Ambience Notes

Rating: ☆☆☆☆☆

Drinks/Cocktails Notes

Rating: ☆☆☆☆☆

Appetizer Notes

....

....

....

....

....

Rating: ☆☆☆☆☆

Main Course Notes

....

....

....

....

....

Rating: ☆☆☆☆☆

Desserts Note

....

....

....

....

....

Rating: ☆☆☆☆☆

Restaurant Name:

....

Location/Address:

....

Contact Details/Social Media:

....

Cuisine/Type Of Food:

....

Dined With:

....

Signature Dishes:

....

Ambience Notes

....

....

....

....

....

Rating: ☆☆☆☆☆

Drinks/Cocktails Notes

....

....

....

....

....

Rating: ☆☆☆☆☆

Appetizer Notes

....

....

....

....

....

Rating: ☆☆☆☆☆

Main Course Notes

....

....

....

....

....

Rating: ☆☆☆☆☆

Desserts Note

....

....

....

....

....

Rating: ☆☆☆☆☆

Restaurant Name:

Location/Address:

Contact Details/Social Media:

Cuisine/Type Of Food:

Dined With:

Signature Dishes:

Ambience Notes

Rating: ☆☆☆☆☆

Drinks/Cocktails Notes

Rating: ☆☆☆☆☆

Appetizer Notes

....

....

....

....

....

Rating: 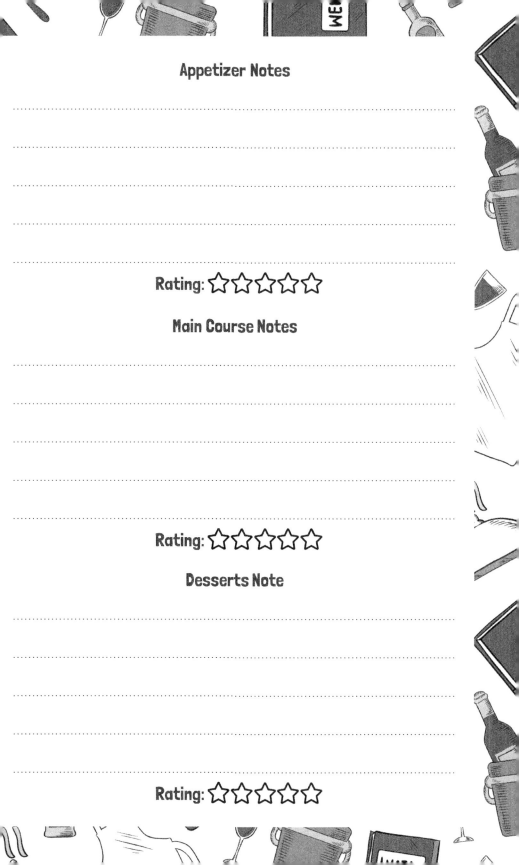 ☆☆☆☆☆

Main Course Notes

....

....

....

....

....

Rating: ☆☆☆☆☆

Desserts Note

....

....

....

....

....

Rating: ☆☆☆☆☆

Restaurant Name:

Location/Address:

Contact Details/Social Media:

Cuisine/Type Of Food:

Dined With:

Signature Dishes:

Ambience Notes

Rating: ☆☆☆☆☆

Drinks/Cocktails Notes

Rating: ☆☆☆☆☆

Appetizer Notes

....

....

....

....

....

Rating: ☆☆☆☆☆

Main Course Notes

....

....

....

....

....

Rating: ☆☆☆☆☆

Desserts Note

....

....

....

....

....

Rating: ☆☆☆☆☆

Restaurant Name:

Location/Address:

Contact Details/Social Media:

Cuisine/Type Of Food:

Dined With:

Signature Dishes:

Ambience Notes

Rating: ☆☆☆☆☆

Drinks/Cocktails Notes

Rating: ☆☆☆☆☆

Appetizer Notes

....

....

....

....

Rating: ☆☆☆☆☆

Main Course Notes

....

....

....

....

Rating: ☆☆☆☆☆

Desserts Note

....

....

....

....

....

Rating: ☆☆☆☆☆

Restaurant Name:

Location/Address:

Contact Details/Social Media:

Cuisine/Type Of Food:

Dined With:

Signature Dishes:

Ambience Notes

Rating: ☆☆☆☆☆

Drinks/Cocktails Notes

Rating: ☆☆☆☆☆

Appetizer Notes

....

....

....

....

....

Rating: ☆☆☆☆☆

Main Course Notes

....

....

....

....

....

Rating: ☆☆☆☆☆

Desserts Note

....

....

....

....

....

Rating: ☆☆☆☆☆

Restaurant Name:

Location/Address:

Contact Details/Social Media:

Cuisine/Type Of Food:

Dined With:

Signature Dishes:

Ambience Notes

Rating: ☆☆☆☆☆

Drinks/Cocktails Notes

Rating: ☆☆☆☆☆

Appetizer Notes

....

....

....

....

....

Rating: ☆☆☆☆☆

Main Course Notes

....

....

....

....

....

Rating: ☆☆☆☆☆

Desserts Note

....

....

....

....

....

Rating: ☆☆☆☆☆

Restaurant Name:

Location/Address:

Contact Details/Social Media:

Cuisine/Type Of Food:

Dined With:

Signature Dishes:

Ambience Notes

Rating: ☆☆☆☆☆

Drinks/Cocktails Notes

Rating: ☆☆☆☆☆

Appetizer Notes

....

....

....

....

....

Rating: ☆☆☆☆☆

Main Course Notes

....

....

....

....

....

Rating: ☆☆☆☆☆

Desserts Note

....

....

....

....

....

Rating: ☆☆☆☆☆

Restaurant Name:

Location/Address:

Contact Details/Social Media:

Cuisine/Type Of Food:

Dined With:

Signature Dishes:

Ambience Notes

Rating: ☆☆☆☆☆

Drinks/Cocktails Notes

Rating: ☆☆☆☆☆

Appetizer Notes

....

....

....

....

....

Rating: ☆☆☆☆☆

Main Course Notes

....

....

....

....

....

Rating: ☆☆☆☆☆

Desserts Note

....

....

....

....

....

Rating: ☆☆☆☆☆

Restaurant Name:

Location/Address:

Contact Details/Social Media:

Cuisine/Type Of Food:

Dined With:

Signature Dishes:

Ambience Notes

Rating: ☆☆☆☆☆

Drinks/Cocktails Notes

Rating: ☆☆☆☆☆

Appetizer Notes

....

....

....

....

....

Rating: ☆☆☆☆☆

Main Course Notes

....

....

....

....

....

Rating: ☆☆☆☆☆

Desserts Note

....

....

....

....

....

Rating: ☆☆☆☆☆

Restaurant Name:

Location/Address:

Contact Details/Social Media:

Cuisine/Type Of Food:

Dined With:

Signature Dishes:

Ambience Notes

Rating: ☆☆☆☆☆

Drinks/Cocktails Notes

Rating: ☆☆☆☆☆

Appetizer Notes

....

....

....

....

Rating: ☆☆☆☆☆

Main Course Notes

....

....

....

....

Rating: ☆☆☆☆☆

Desserts Note

....

....

....

....

....

Rating: ☆☆☆☆☆

Restaurant Name:

Location/Address:

Contact Details/Social Media:

Cuisine/Type Of Food:

Dined With:

Signature Dishes:

Ambience Notes

Rating: ☆☆☆☆☆

Drinks/Cocktails Notes

Rating: ☆☆☆☆☆

Appetizer Notes

....

....

....

....

....

Rating: ☆☆☆☆☆

Main Course Notes

....

....

....

....

....

Rating: ☆☆☆☆☆

Desserts Note

....

....

....

....

....

Rating: ☆☆☆☆☆

Restaurant Name:

Location/Address:

Contact Details/Social Media:

Cuisine/Type Of Food:

Dined With:

Signature Dishes:

Ambience Notes

Rating: ☆☆☆☆☆

Drinks/Cocktails Notes

Rating: ☆☆☆☆☆

Appetizer Notes

....

....

....

....

....

Rating: ☆☆☆☆☆

Main Course Notes

....

....

....

....

....

Rating: ☆☆☆☆☆

Desserts Note

....

....

....

....

....

Rating: ☆☆☆☆☆

Restaurant Name:

Location/Address:

Contact Details/Social Media:

Cuisine/Type Of Food:

Dined With:

Signature Dishes:

Ambience Notes

Rating: ☆☆☆☆☆

Drinks/Cocktails Notes

Rating: ☆☆☆☆☆

Appetizer Notes

....

....

....

....

....

Rating: ☆☆☆☆☆

Main Course Notes

....

....

....

....

....

Rating: ☆☆☆☆☆

Desserts Note

....

....

....

....

....

Rating: ☆☆☆☆☆

Restaurant Name:

Location/Address:

Contact Details/Social Media:

Cuisine/Type Of Food:

Dined With:

Signature Dishes:

Ambience Notes

Rating: ☆☆☆☆☆

Drinks/Cocktails Notes

Rating: ☆☆☆☆☆

Appetizer Notes

....

....

....

....

....

Rating: ☆☆☆☆☆

Main Course Notes

....

....

....

....

....

Rating: ☆☆☆☆☆

Desserts Note

....

....

....

....

....

Rating: ☆☆☆☆☆

Restaurant Name:

Location/Address:

Contact Details/Social Media:

Cuisine/Type Of Food:

Dined With:

Signature Dishes:

Ambience Notes

Rating: ☆☆☆☆☆

Drinks/Cocktails Notes

Rating: ☆☆☆☆☆

Appetizer Notes

....

....

....

....

....

Rating: ☆☆☆☆☆

Main Course Notes

....

....

....

....

....

Rating: ☆☆☆☆☆

Desserts Note

....

....

....

....

....

Rating: ☆☆☆☆☆

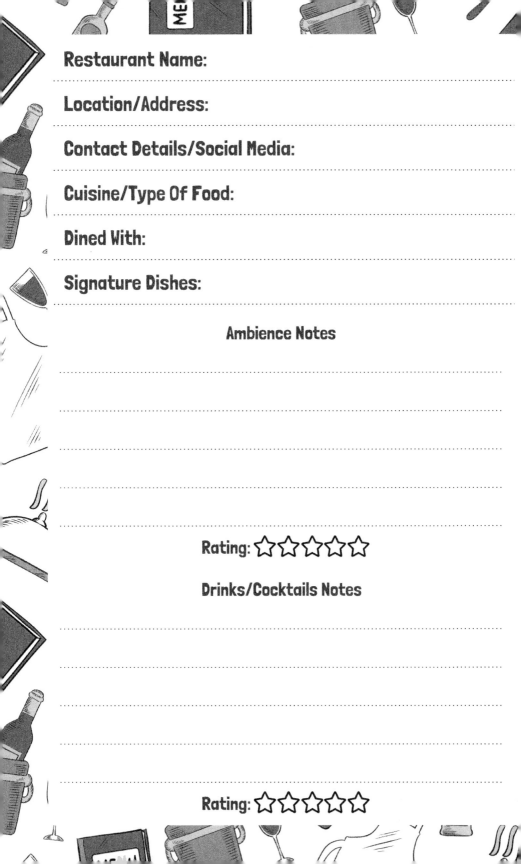

Restaurant Name:

Location/Address:

Contact Details/Social Media:

Cuisine/Type Of Food:

Dined With:

Signature Dishes:

Ambience Notes

Rating: ☆☆☆☆☆

Drinks/Cocktails Notes

Rating: ☆☆☆☆☆

Appetizer Notes

....

....

....

....

....

Rating: ☆☆☆☆☆

Main Course Notes

....

....

....

....

....

Rating: ☆☆☆☆☆

Desserts Note

....

....

....

....

....

Rating: ☆☆☆☆☆

Restaurant Name:

Location/Address:

Contact Details/Social Media:

Cuisine/Type Of Food:

Dined With:

Signature Dishes:

Ambience Notes

Rating: ☆☆☆☆☆

Drinks/Cocktails Notes

Rating: ☆☆☆☆☆

Appetizer Notes

....

....

....

....

....

Rating: ☆☆☆☆☆

Main Course Notes

....

....

....

....

....

Rating: ☆☆☆☆☆

Desserts Note

....

....

....

....

....

Rating: ☆☆☆☆☆

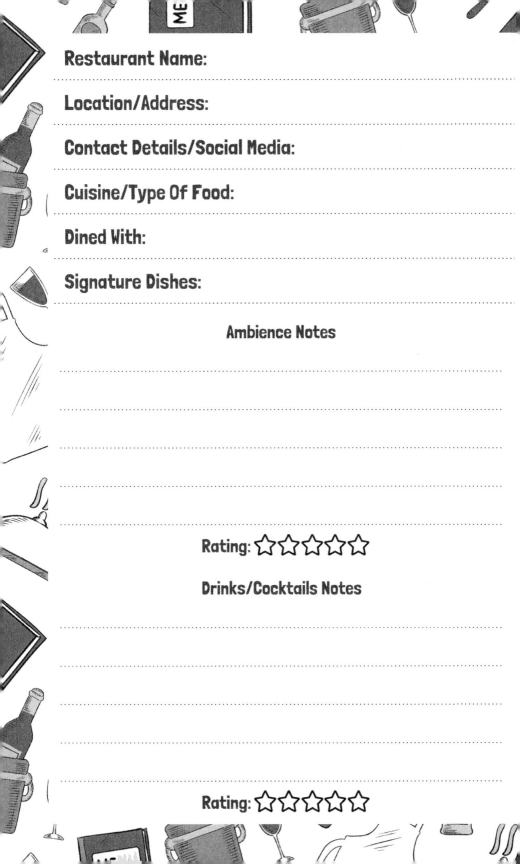

Restaurant Name:

Location/Address:

Contact Details/Social Media:

Cuisine/Type Of Food:

Dined With:

Signature Dishes:

Ambience Notes

Rating: ☆☆☆☆☆

Drinks/Cocktails Notes

Rating: ☆☆☆☆☆

Appetizer Notes

....

....

....

....

....

Rating: ☆☆☆☆☆

Main Course Notes

....

....

....

....

....

Rating: ☆☆☆☆☆

Desserts Note

....

....

....

....

....

Rating: ☆☆☆☆☆

Printed in Great Britain
by Amazon

72641828R00068